DEDICATION

I dedicate this book to cancer patients and survivors, and their family members, friends, and the clinical caregivers supporting their healing journeys. This book's poems speak to the spiritual dimension of the cancer experience. They remind us to nourish our spirits and souls during the cancer journey. The well-known spiritual psychology author, Thomas Moore, reminds us what happens when we ignore our souls. He said, *"When soul is neglected, it doesn't just go away; it appears symptomatically in obsessions, addictions, violence, and loss of meaning."* The message of *Cancer as Spiritual Teacher* is clear: Let's not ignore our souls during the cancer journey. Rather, let's invite our souls to lead us in a healing way along this journey.

Don Iannone

ACKNOWLEDGMENTS

"Cancer as Spiritual Teacher" was inspired by my personal cancer journey and my complementary medicine work with cancer patients at Cleveland Clinic's Taussig Cancer Institute, in partnership with my wife Mary. Poetry promotes healing by surfacing deep emotions, sparking self-awareness and insight, and connecting us with our soul's wisdom. Spiritual healing awaits us in this place. Cancer patients and survivors and their care partners deserve a book of poetry that speaks to the spiritual dimension of their journeys. That's what this book provides.

Mary and I wish to express our gratitude to our family members and friends, some of whom are cancer survivors, who uplifted us during my cancer journey in 2018. We deeply appreciate their love, kindness, thoughtfulness, positivity, and prayers. We are stronger because of their support.

Because of the remarkable medical care provided to me at Cleveland Clinic by Dr. Harry "Bud" Isaacson, M.D., and Dr. Eric A. Klein, M.D., I am a cancer survivor. For their care, Mary and I are deeply grateful.

Finally, Mary and I wish to express our appreciation to Kim Bell, Chief Administrative Officer of Taussig Cancer Institute, for the opportunity to work since 2017 with cancer patients and their care partners at Taussig. It has been an incredibly rich and rewarding experience for both of us.

CONTENTS

"Cancer as Spiritual Teacher" transcends the traditional boundaries of a literary work by weaving together a collection of poems that delve into the multifaceted cancer journey. This compilation does more than just narrate the trials and tribulations faced by those touched by cancer; it explores the profound spiritual awakening and insights that often accompany this challenging path. Each poem serves as a source of light, illuminating the depths of vulnerability, resilience, and the quest for meaning amidst the uncertainty of illness. The inclusion of analyses of the structure, imagery, and meaning of selected poems further enriches the reader's engagement, inviting a deeper contemplation of the layers and nuances embedded within the verses. These examinations highlight the artistry of the poems and also unravel the truths and emotional landscapes encapsulated in the cancer experience. Through this introspective journey, the book champions poetry as a powerful medium for expression and healing, resonating with readers on a profound level.

Beyond its literary contributions, "Cancer as Spiritual Teacher" offers an overview of cancer trends and care care within the U.S., presenting a holistic view of the disease's impact on individuals and the healthcare system. This contextual backdrop sets the stage for an argument for integrating poetry and poetry therapy into medicine, particularly in cancer care. The book identifies the therapeutic benefits of poetry, showcasing how this expressive art form can serve as a vital complement to conventional medical treatments. By facilitating emotional release, fostering a sense of connection, and empowering patients to articulate their innermost thoughts and feelings, poetry therapy emerges as a transformative tool in the healing process. The poetry therapy section underscores the significance of incorporating the humanities into patient care but also reinforces the book's central premise: that within the heartbreak of cancer, there lies an unparalleled opportunity for spiritual growth and discovery. Finally, a glossary of terms is found at the end of the book.

FOREWORD

"Cancer as a Spiritual Teacher" is an honest and empathetic anthology of poems, capturing the essence of fortitude and spirituality found on the path through cancer. It invites us to embrace this illness as a spiritual voyage, paralleling the revered pilgrimage of Spain's Camino de Santiago, where every step is a testament to inner strength and a search for deeper existential meaning.

Drawing from the same spirit that guides the pilgrims of the Camino de Santiago, "Cancer as a Spiritual Teacher" suggests a kindred journey for those facing cancer, one reaching into the depths of the soul. This collection offers poems that encourage readers to walk this path with openness, strength, and gratitude, focusing on healing that goes beyond the physical. These verses inspire inner change, helping readers to recognize and appreciate the spiritual lessons that are part of their cancer journey, leading to personal growth and understanding.

I have been a poet for many years. This second edition of "Cancer as Spiritual Teacher" is my tenth poetry book. I am also a cancer survivor. Interestingly, I began work on this book three months before I was diagnosed with prostate cancer. Since my radical prostatectomy at Cleveland Clinic in July 2018, I have begun my pilgrimage along the El Camino del Cáncer—A path that has been filled with learning, uncertainty, fear, pain, spiritual insight, love, gratitude, and healing. My cancer experience has challenged my deepest beliefs about life and death, and what happens in between the two. This book speaks to how I am working with these challenges spiritually.

One early conclusion I made is that my life will always be larger than my cancer. I know also that my life has given rise to my cancer—A reality for all of us with cancer. Through my work with cancer patients at the Cleveland Clinic, I understand the monumental demands cancer places on the lives of patients and their families. I have also learned that cancer healing requires us to put our cancer into a larger life perspective, which is possible by developing a spiritual understanding of our cancer.

The Trappist monk Thomas Merton said, "If you want to identify me, ask me not where I live, or what I like to eat, or how I comb my hair, but ask me what I am living for, in detail, ask me what I think is keeping me from living fully for the thing I want to live for." This book's poems speak to what I am living for.

While the initial inspiration for this book came from the Reiki and meditation services that my wife Mary and I provide to cancer patients, many of the poems written after my cancer diagnosis reflect my deeper personal thoughts and feelings about cancer. The poems in this book hold even greater meaning for me now as a cancer survivor.

Cancer is a spiritual teacher for me. It can be the same for you. Like all cancer survivors, I want to be cured and never have to worry again about cancer. I also want to grow personally and spiritually from my cancer experience. I am a spiritual being, and so are you, because spirit makes up the core of our beings. Cancer is a test of my ability as a spiritual alchemist to turn lead (cancer) into gold (spiritual growth). Your cancer can represent the same for you.

Healing is about achieving greater wholeness by improving our everyday life balance and spiritual alignment. It is also about replacing our conditioned fear and mistrust of the universe's intentions for us with greater openness, trust, deeper understanding, and increased confidence and courage. Fear, anxiety, and anger—three of our most commonly misdirected emotional energies—have roots in our misunderstanding of the true nature of reality, which is inherently creative, uncertain, fluid, and impermanent, and yet deeply loving by design. In this context, love is the connective force in the universe that transcends our experiences of separation from our spiritual essence. Love is who we are and how we are in the world when we feel our life force connection to ourselves, others, the universe, and God.

As creatures of habit, we "condition" ourselves to live in the world in programmed ways. At times, our conditioning works well for us, and at other times, it fails us miserably. Fear, anxiety, and anger are deeply conditioned ways in which we perceive reality, and act in the world in line with these perceptions. All three of these emotions create "war zones" in our bodies, minds, and spirits. In this light, it is little wonder that many cancer patients and survivors, and those who support them, decide to "declare war on cancer," which in my judgment can create even greater imbalance, disharmony, confusion, and separation—All of which undermine our systemic health and well-being. This book urges us to see the cancer journey as a spiritual healing pilgrimage, rather than a war we declare on diseased parts of our body. Not everyone will agree with this alternative path. It is for each of us to decide the path we should walk in dealing with cancer.

We need this book in the world because it creates an awareness of how our spiritual conflict and crisis, psychic pain, toxic emotions, and life traumas set the stage for and catalyze cancer growth in our bodies. These factors contribute to cancer growth, perhaps as much so as our genetic endowments, the environments in which we live, and our daily lifestyles. As souls with bodies, rather than bodies with souls, spiritual realities ultimately determine the course of our lives. Mind, spirit, and our consciousness are major determinants of our physical health and well-being, and we shouldn't discount their importance.

Western science-based medicine has advanced its abilities to detect and destroy cancer cells, and to an increasing degree predict where cancer may develop, and who could develop cancer. Yet, scientists and medical professionals have not arrived at a clear, universally accepted definition of cancer and its causes. We cannot understand cancer in our bodies in isolation from our minds and spirits, which argues for a "spiritually based integrative medicine" to prevent and treat cancer through whole-person healing modalities. The poems in this book help us visualize and embrace this new integrative healing path.

As I look at my life, I am reminded of the words of the bestselling author and spiritual teacher Eckhart Tolle, who said, "Life will give you whatever experience is most helpful for the evolution of your consciousness. How do you know this is the experience you need? Because this is the experience you are having at the moment." Cancer is an opportunity to evolve my consciousness and grow spiritually. I accept it as a teacher of the spiritual wisdom at this point in my life. The poems in this book can help you do the same.

Cancer is not a teacher anyone would invite into their life, yet it can be a powerful teacher. Our spirits need nourishment as we walk the cancer healing path. "Cancer as Spiritual Teacher" encourages us to contemplate our situation in life, including our darkest days and nights, open to our naturally loving spirits, and allow healing to occur on all levels of our being.

This book is a tapestry of my spiritual insights, woven from a diverse array of religious and philosophical threads from around the globe. It's not just the traditions that have shaped my thoughts; it's also the deep dives into human consciousness, the mysteries unraveled by quantum physics, and the explorations of philosophy. I find joy and wisdom in poetry and photography, and they too, have colored my spiritual canvas.

Every day, I sit in mindfulness meditation, finding peace in the stillness, and I turn to creative expression as my gateway to spiritual depth. Crafting this book has been more than just writing; it's been a journey of healing, a way to mend and grow spiritually.

As you delve into the verses within these pages, let them resonate with your innermost being. Let the words flow into your heart and spirit, guiding you on your personal journey of healing and peace. I hope that the messages enclosed will touch you, offering comfort, love, and empathy.

CANCER AS SPIRITUAL TEACHER

CANCER AS SPIRITUAL TEACHER

*Poems on Walking
the Healing Path*

DONALD T. IANNONE

Wisdom Work Press

ABOUT THIS COLLECTION

This section of the book brings together a collection of poems that touch on different aspects of the cancer journey. These poems come from my own experiences with cancer, as well as from my work with cancer patients and their families. Through these verses, I hope to share insights into the emotional and spiritual dimensions of facing cancer.

My personal journey with cancer has taught me a lot, not just about the disease, but also about resilience, hope, and the complex emotions that come with such a diagnosis. The poems I've written from this part of my life aim to capture these feelings and reflections, hoping they might offer some comfort or understanding to others going through similar situations. Many of these poems reflect in non-confidential ways the stories shared with me by cancer patients and their family members. Their experiences, diverse and impactful, contribute to a broader understanding of what it means to live with cancer. Their stories speak to the shared challenges and the unique paths of those affected by this illness.

Central to these poems is the role of spirituality in the cancer journey. For many, spirituality provides a source of strength, hope, and peace. It's been an important aspect of my own experience and in the lives of those I've worked with. These poems explore how spirituality can offer support and insights during difficult times. Overall, these poems aim is to connect with readers through shared experiences and insights, offering support and understanding through the medium of poetry.

POEMS IN THIS COLLECTION

> *"Cancer is not merely a journey through the body, but a profound voyage into the depths of the soul, revealing our existential nature. It reminds us that every challenge faced is an opportunity for growth, and every moment of despair is balanced with hope, illuminating the delicate dance between our mortality and our spirit's resilience."*
>
> *~Don Iannone*

On Cancer and Poetry

Battling cancer, we grasp at every straw,
Poetry, too, becomes a healing salve.
It ushers us gently into life's raw thrall,
Cleansing old beliefs in its restorative bath.

Cancer, those rapids wild, looms in our sight,
But we'll navigate its twists with dignity and might.

Poetry, like life, can dangerously entice,
Revealing depths within us, untouched, unknown.
Yet, in the throes of cancer, it's worth the roll of dice,
For in its verses, a transmuting force is shown.

In the dance with cancer, let poetry play its part,
Transforming our trials into triumph, a healing art.

Poetry Connecting Us to Our Spiritual Beings

In these poems it's clear, we're spiritual, it's true,
Loved as we are, through and through.
I've crossed paths with many who've yet to see,
Their spiritual essence, forever free.

We miss life's grandeur if we fail to find,
Our deeper selves, leaving the surface behind.
These verses beckon, step out, explore,
Our life, our illness, and so much more.

Close your eyes, let your heart's door sway,
To glimpse the bright Light that shows the way.
This Light from our soul, a beacon so bold,
Guides our steps on this journey we hold.

Each poem, a wave on the sea's grand scale,
Bringing us home as we set sail.

Life's Fragileness

our lives hang
by
a delicately woven
string,
sheathed in life's
promises,
broken by cancer
cells.

Sunrise Whispers

Sunrise whispers atop the sleepy knoll.
An embrace we feel in our soul.
Sad you say, so little control.
Ardent travelers, through life we stroll.
From one day to the next, we make our way.

Deeper places these whispers bring.
Clouds like islands in the sky,
And to them, I try my best to cling.
For just a while longer I wish to sing.
More sunrise whispers, please, before I die.

Each day its share of light and dark,
And so much more in between.
Lasting memories sunrise colors spark.
From life, death does embark,
And from embattled cells, cancer grows.

Without fanfare, or desperate provocation,
By the frosted window, I sit watching
This morning's divine creation.
And in my heart lies undying adoration
At the way sunrise whispers its sweet melodies.

Life Between Our Plans

Remember when you were ten,
and thought at twenty-one,
you'd be all grown up and perfectly happy?
Then, when you were thirteen,
your father died of a sudden heart attack,
and your family nearly fell apart.

Remember when you were twenty-one,
and thought at forty,
you'd have life all figured out?
Then, just as you finished college at twenty-two,
you became pregnant with your first daughter Lauren,
and your plans to become a trial lawyer came to an end.

Remember when you were forty-five,
and all three kids were on their own,
and you thought you could launch your writing career?
Then, two days after your first book was accepted,
your mother was diagnosed with Alzheimer's,
and all your life energy shifted to caring for her.

Remember when you were sixty-five,
had published eight books, and you thought
you and your husband Tom could relax and smell the roses?
Then, when you were sixty-seven,

Tom died after a prolonged battle with cancer,
and Lauren entered rehab for drug abuse.

Remember just yesterday, on your eighty-third birthday,
you marveled at how life seems to happen
in between all the plans we make?
Nothing could be truer.

Under the Shadows

Something wild rages,
just out of reach of the sun's touch,
and beyond the moon's chilling lost call.
Within us, an unknown wildness arises.

And down below, and beyond,
incarnate spirits walk the shadows
in search of what the wildness brings.
Their forms soon to change.

And in those shadows,
the empty hollows fill with twilight's wonders,
and silence clings to misplaced souls,
like lingering dreams to our first waking breaths.

And should danger appear, please remember:
He that dwelleth in the secret place
of the most High shall abide
under the shadow of the Almighty.

Note: Last stanza from Psalms 91:1

Poems on Love

On Love #1

Love is the rain
that cleanses,
refreshes, and washes away
the non-essentials in our lives.

On Love #2

Love is what comes most naturally to us,
connecting us with our higher being.
Love is God's Light shining brightly within us.

On Love #3

What is love?
Love is our true nature.
Love is what makes us whole.

On Love #4

Love anchors us.
Love frees us.
We are love.

Life and Death: Two Sides of the Same Quantum Coin

Life and death–
Two sides of the same quantum coin.
Heads you win, tails you lose.
Call the flip.
Tails you win, heads you lose.
Call it again.

Life–
What our consciousness manifests
when we flip the coin.
Death–
What our consciousness manifests
when we flip the coin.

Life and death–
Two sides of the same quantum coin.

Experiencing the Speed of Life

Pay attention to life's details,
especially the infinitesimally small things
that bring you happiness and joy.
Marvel at how quickly each moment passes by
with each breath you take.
This is the speed of life.

Experience the surprise in everything.
Don't prejudge what's to come.
Notice how no two moments are the same,
like snowflakes or grains of sand.
This is you—
An ever-changing wave of possibility.

Gratitude for the Rain

I am thankful for my life–
just the way it is.
It's easy to forget–
life is one great miracle,
and each of us has had the chance
to experience life's wonder and magic.

On this rainy Thursday morning,
I am grateful for the rain,
and how it nourishes and cleanses the earth.
Without it, there would be no flowers.
In a soulful way, the rain reminds us it is okay
for us to cry tears of joy and sorrow.

Because of the rain this morning,
I can see the world reflected
in a single raindrop dangling
from the screen in my front window.
In this moment, I give thanks for the rain,
and the blessings it brings to my life.

Breaking Ego's Hold

Ego servants, you and me,
To things we love, can't get free,
Ensnared are we by selfish pride,
Forgetting that, in God we abide.

So much energy oft gets spent,
In things propelling our descent,
In things focused just on you and me,
Nothing left for humanity.

Habits learned over a lifetime,
Worsen yet in our prime,
For it is then, we're at the top,
Afraid we are, bad habits to stop.

Off course at times, we steer our ship,
Hard it is to get a firm grip,
And change our proud and selfish side,
The dark parts of us, we cannot hide.

Because it's hard, that's no excuse,
Around our necks remains the noose,
While no easy answers within our reach,
Each day we must practice what we preach.

"Last Time" Awareness

The world looks different to us
with the awareness that
this may be the last time
we will ever see it.

At these times,
goodbyes, no matter how grand,
appreciative, or reverent,
ring with lingering hollowness.

And memories, even the most precious,
become bitter two-edged swords,
reminding us of what we loved,
and what we will never see again.

Even the deepest understanding
of reality's impermanent nature
doesn't prevent us from grasping at
what we love, and what has given us joy.

A Prayer Honoring Our Wholeness

In this moment, I am whole.
All parts of me are working together
to promote healing and well-being.
My body receives wisdom from my mind and spirit.
My mind is given embodiment from my body, and
life force energy from my spirit.
My spirit permeates all I am, and
it is the source of my future possibilities.
With each breath, I am connected to God.
I am thankful for my wholeness.

Soulful Advice on Living

Don't punish yourself
with unnecessary prognostications
about the time of your death.
For your death, like my death,
will come soon enough.

Live as best you can,
for as long as you can.
Let love be your path,
and hope be your guide.
Now is your time, live it well.

Cancer's No Joke, but It's Okay to Laugh

Laughter won't kill me, so why not bust a gut?
No harm in a chortled snicker or a devious snort
at the prissy old lady in the room next door
who punctuated the air with a loud squeaky fart.
Sitting with my bags in the northwest corner chemo suite,
I heard a nurse exclaim: Dunkin' Donuts can't be beat.
Then, in unison I heard everyone sigh:
the donuts are gone, so sad we could cry.

Almost peed my pants, laughing so hard,
when a senior oncologist let down his guard—
sharing advice with a young resident doctor;
straight from Mother Goose, my what a shocker:
"For every evil under the sun,
There is a remedy, or there is none.
If there be one, seek till you find it;
And when you find it, get thee behind it."

A ride in the elevator, so very telling about life,
Shall I smoke a joint before chemo, a man asks his wife,
A punch in his chest she landed with might,
I feared at that moment there could be a fight.
I urge you to give humor a chance,
Let jokes and laughter enliven your life dance,
Some craziness at times all of us need,
Laugh at yourself, start a healing stampede.

Our Stations in Life

Stations in life:
Places we find ourselves,
often where we least expect to be.
Positions we assume,
unknowingly and otherwise.

Parts of our journey—
sometimes journeys within journeys.
When we're properly tuned in,
our stations offer a pivotal view
of what we need to see and do.

A place for seeing, and sometimes
escaping what we don't wish to see.

As simple as looking into another person's eyes,
reflecting on a conversation,
giving up what we believe, and
ultimately letting go of one station,
without knowing the next one ahead.

Hard Things to Imagine

Hard to imagine
being dead,
since all we know
is being alive.

Hard to imagine
life after death,
since all we know
is being alive.

Hard to imagine
dreaming of things
beyond our experience,
but we do this every day.

Hard to imagine
when we're dead and gone,
absent any reason to remember,
that our dreams bring us back to life.

On Being Present

Don't look back, you'll only see
a faint, disappearing reality.
Your past may beckon, set it free.
Things behind you, let them be.

Ahead of you, the future lies.
Much to come, a surprise.
Look ahead, if you will,
but careful not the present kill.

Always in the now you are.
Dangling even, from afar.
Soon enough, the future comes.
Now again, it becomes.

Time escapes all of us.
In between, no need to fuss.
No matter where you're sent,
try your best, be fully present.

Truth as Your Surgical Knife

Psychic surgery—
You're the surgeon.
Cut carefully,
removing only the bad,
leaving the good.

Some parts of us look diseased,
needing extrication, but
at a closer inspection, we see
good and bad sewn together.
All parts of the same cloth.

Parts and wholes,
just illusions:
things we hate,
and things we love—
All parts of who we are.

Surgery, on one level,
separating us, parceling out
what's not needed
to be healthy
and grow stronger.

Should you decide
psychic surgery is required
to heal yourself,
choose truth as the knife
to remove what's no longer needed.

We Can Conquer Our Fear

We can conquer our fear–of cancer,
the pain it causes,
sometimes even the sting of death.

Fear feeds our cancer–
causes it to mushroom larger than life.
Let's do our best, and
snuff out the cancer flame.

The starting point:
feel our deepest fear,
get to know its name,
and then, let it dissolve away.

Cancer—There can be worse things.
Fear—A sign to deepen our trust
of times when the house grows dark,
and the shadows overstep the light.

Reality by nature, serving up
hard questions with no easy answers.
Certainty, just abject illusions,
holding what we fear at bay.

We have but this moment,

at any point in our lives.
Let's choose to live fearlessly,
savoring each breath we take.

Hope

Hope is the ground we walk on,
the air we breathe, and
the water quenching our deepest thirst
to be alive.

Hope is essential for our healing,
providing the wings
helping us to fly,
carrying us past our pain.

Never lose hope, because
it is a lasting gift,
given to us
by our souls.

Who Are We?

If we are not who we think we are,
then who are we?
We are that which comes before
who we think we are.

You and I are sentient beings,
witnessing reality's unfolding
in each breath we take.
I am that, and you are that.

Acceptance

Agnes, a mere nineteen springs, her journey's span,
Since sixteen, faced a trial no one plans.
Her smile, a beacon, pure without pretense,
Shows us the power of choice's immense.

To embrace what is, and live it true,
Or veil our eyes, and deny the view.
Her laughter, a choice in reality's dance,
She lives each moment, not leaving it to chance.

Let's learn from her, in sun or rain,
To live fully, through joy or pain.

Cancer as Spiritual Teacher

In every life, lessons are sown,
Truths to unearth, to make our own.
Some are simple, like recipes to taste,
Others, complex, not one bit of waste.

Our souls may shout from depths of pain,
But from such trials, wisdom's what we gain.
With open hearts and minds to blend,
New paths appear, old ways we mend.

To learn from cancer, a task so stark,
Yet within its shadows, a divine spark.
It's a dance of balance, a call to find
Our truest selves, in heart and mind.

The lessons I've learned, humbly so:
To let fear and ego gracefully go.
To tread a path where trust is a must,
And love guides my steps, in the divine I trust.

Cancer is more than its physical trace,
It holds lessons deep, for us to embrace.
With clarity and courage, let's each find,
In spiritual truth, peace of mind.

Thoughts While Watering the Grass This Morning

Cancer reminds us of things in life we take for granted,
like the simple beauty of watering the grass.
It reminds us of all the small things comprising our lives,
and why and how they are important to us.

It calls our attention to life's intricate details,
including the trillions of cells in our body,
and how misguided cells can grow and multiply,
waging war on the better parts of who we are.

Cancer teaches us to constantly nourish ourselves,
like we weed and water our yard and garden,
to bring about personal health and vitality,
and help the right things to flourish in our lives.

And when we are ready,
cancer can connect us to our inner wisdom—
those lessons our souls want us to learn,
aligning our lives with our true destinies.

Where Mind is the Creator

In a world
where mind is the creator,
cancer isn't the problem.
The problem is
what we think, feel, and do.

How we live our lives,
the relationships we form and
what they lead us to become,
give rise to the health
of our bodies, minds, and spirits.

On Life's Beauty

Some days I think I can.
Some days I think I can't.
On days I can,
Life seems so beautiful.
On days I can't,
Life seems even more beautiful.

Hanging in Pristine Nakedness

Too often, too much.
At times, not enough.
Then, when we're satisfied,
something new arises,
moving us, to yet another new place,

Usually a place we'd never find, unless
the world slows down enough,
letting us catch up,
letting us surpass ourselves,
and find more truth than lies.

More solid, dependable ground we need
rather than earthquake-shaken soil,
undermining our hope,
dumping us headlong
onto the beach of time.

And then, the beach disappears,
and all her sand is gone,
we're left, hanging
like the new moon,
in pristine nakedness before sunrise.

Cancer Lesson on Empathy and Caring

Cancer can be a powerful teacher,
if we allow it to be.
One lesson it teaches:
Healing is a shared journey,
with those we love, and
with other cancer survivors.

When attacked, self-preservation is our first instinct.
That's fine, as long as we have empathy for others.
What we think and feel has everything to do
with what happens to our bodies.
A lack of caring for ourselves and others
is a spark reigniting cancer fires.

Lighting a Prayer Candle

Our hearts are warmed when a far-off friend
expresses prayerful intentions for us
by lighting a candle in his parish,
symbolizing his prayer for our healing.

Each of us is a candle lit at birth by God.
And we grow in His favor
when we use our candle to light others,
and dispel darkness in the world.

Cellular Wisdom

Each human cell, a storehouse of wisdom.
Unique among its thirty-five trillion counterparts,
yet aligned with its own special star in the universe,
and programmed from the beginning
to play its role in sustaining the whole
through oneness of purpose and action.
Trust your cellular wisdom.

Our Lives as Quantum Questions

Let's not make unwarranted assumptions in life,
because they block our natural spiritual unfolding.
Far better to allow open questions to linger,
until they are ready to answer themselves.

Each of us is a living question, and
we remain alive as long as our question lingers.
Our questions ride quantum waves of possibility,
until they become answers, then they cease to exist.

Our Scars

Let's be truthful about our scars in life,
and how we got them.
They're not just about physical injuries and pain–
Our scars reflect how we've lived our lives.

Sometimes we learn more from our scars
than the stripes we wear on our sleeves,
or all the awards we've won.
Let's be truthful about our scars in life.

We are capable of healing,
but not always in the way we hope.
Healing deeply inside is most important–
These scars tell the real stories of our lives

Reiki with Cancer Patients

Touching their bodies with Reiki,
reaching deep down into their souls.

Bringing comfort through gentle touch,
sparking greater vital energy flow.

Healing through balance and wholeness—
the best medicine we can ever find.

Generating warmth with our hands,
knowing life itself is the greatest miracle.

Realizing each of us can give peace to others,
through healing touch and loving presence.

Finding a Cure

Chloe's eight.
Sweet child, lovely smile,
eternal optimism, and
stage-four cancer
in her brain and spine.

No, it's not fair, and
Chloe knows that,
but she still believes in miracles,
and hasn't given up.
Nor should we.

Look into her sparkling brown eyes;
so much life speaking through them,
telling us there's something more powerful
than the hideous beast
feeding on her precious life energy.

In all this,
so much unexpected hope
from what seems so hopeless.
From all this,
life becomes even more precious.

Soul-Searching

There are times when
we feel our impermanence–
that unhinging inner sense
we cannot live forever.

Our journeys begin,
searching for our souls—
that elusive river of light
from which everything flows.

Our journeys then plunge deeper within—
to that beautiful flower of truth,
whose seeds give birth
to our presence each day.

Our souls beckon us
in each breath we take,
inviting our deep questions—
those making us feel most alive.

Suffering Greater Than Cancer

Cut short–
lives ravaged by cancer.
But for some, a grand escape
from deeper life suffering.

Jigsaw Puzzles in the Cancer Treatment Waiting Room

Jigsaw puzzles, missing pieces everywhere,
That patients, families, and friends share.
Some they finish, most they don't,
Some too hard, so they won't.

Oddly shaped interlocking and tessellating pieces.
Bit by bit, the perplexing mystery decreases.
Skilled puzzlers work first to build the frame,
While others treat all pieces exactly the same.

Some work the puzzles like their lives,
Trying this, trying that, till an answer arrives.
While befuddled by the jigsaw puzzles,
Cancer causes much bigger struggles.

For some, the puzzles distract them from their pain.
Others wonder about life on the celestial plane.
When finally, the nurse calls their name,
In the waiting room, the jigsaw puzzles remain.

On the First Day of December

Six years ago,
On the first day of December,
My life flashed before my eyes,
Like nothing I can remember.

Things I used to take for granted:
My work, the kids, and my wife,
And even smaller things like morning coffee,
Those things that make up ordinary life.

For months, I ignored the dull aching pain,
Till it spread across my pelvis and lower back,
And then gave way to such sheer agony,
I felt my body battered and under attack.

My doctor ran the usual tests.
All were normal, but for one.
My PSA was way too high.
More tests to be run.

Within days, the wellspring of my misery known:
Stage III prostate cancer, which had spread.
In a flash, radiation, surgery, hormone therapy.
Without of course, I'd be dead.

Since that time, a celebration of life is held,
Come rain or shine, each first day of December.
Each year, month, week, and day,
We dearly cherish and prayerfully remember.

Finding Our Inner Wisdom Voices

Find your inner wisdom voice–
There lies your deepest personal truth.
Listen past your throbbing fears–
They drown out your truth.
Look beyond your anger–
Which often is buried beneath your fear.
Set aside your desires and wants, and listen
to what it takes to become whole and heal.

On Courage and Fear

Courage is acting
in the face of fear, and
doing what must be done,
without knowing
the outcome in advance.

Fear is resisting action
because we see life
in strict win-lose terms, and
we see ourselves as more likely
to lose than to win.

Courage requires us
to see life freely and abundantly,
while fear requires us
to protect ourselves,
rather than grow.

Being courageous doesn't mean
we won't be afraid, and
being afraid doesn't mean
we can't be courageous.
Choose courage over fear!

Learning a New Language

Each of us is unique, you know.
We live our lives, let them flow
as though there is no tomorrow, and
then our cancer says that's no longer so.

One thing you learn right away—
A new language is required to keep death at bay.
So many confounding terms, indecipherable abbreviations—
Things you never imagine anyone would say.

Our doctors, nurses, and other caregivers
never know exactly what cancer delivers,
They give it their best to find the right words,
which often get lost in cancer's fast-moving rivers.

Berlitz can't teach us to speak this tongue.
Requires a doctor, nurse, someone from a technical rung.
We cringe to words like malignant, spread and metastasis,
And words like benign and clear, Heaven's praises sung.

For fear the language of cancer they may abuse,
Cure and healing, rare words that oncologists use.
Instead they dance, tiny delicate ballet steps.
Bolder terms about prognosis they refuse.

But late at night when I talk to God,
I spare no words in asking to be healed.
Anything else just a façade.
Bolder words I use, along the healing path I trod.

Whose Life Is This? I Think I Know

Whose life is that? I think I know.
Its owner scows with anger so.
Standing before the bathroom mirror
As life slips away, death draws nearer.

To himself, he introspects.
Thoughts he seeks and collects.
At times, he blames himself for all this.
The cancer and its hellish abyss.

On better days, he remembers,
Cancer took many family members,
Which in some small way consoles his guilt
That he himself sabotaged the life he built.

Beyond his feelings lies a reality.
A place where he can be free.
Another chance hopefully to start over.
And where cancer has no spillover.

Prayers

Prayer #1

God help us to live in joy and thanksgiving,
to forgive ourselves and others,
heal the sadness and sorrow in our hearts,
know ourselves deeply and fully,
and use our self-knowledge
to bring forth love in the world.

Prayer #2

God help us to see past our blind spots,
including our limited view of you, others, and ourselves.
Forgive us when we don't sacrifice enough for others,
when our compassion falls short,
and when we can only love conditionally.

Forgive us when we don't thank you
for the precious gift of life
you have given us.
Help us use our gifts to honor you
and bring about goodness in the world.

Prayer #3
God forgive us for pulling away from your love,
for failing to see your Divine presence
that sustains us in each moment and every day.

Open our hearts to your love.
Uplift us so we may uplift others.
Let us celebrate your power and beauty in all things.

Prayer #4
God give us the vision to see reality,
and to know the truth in a living way.
Grant us the wisdom
to know ourselves and others
in a loving and kind way.

Help us transcend our pain and suffering
by using them to grow stronger
in compassion and empathy.
Help us see the world in all its beauty
without judgment and attachment.

Help us replace our pride with humility,
and live in a conscious way.
Protect us from our own self-doubt,
ignorance of higher purpose, and
at times underestimating our true potential.

Karmic Wheel

That overlooked, we become,
Tracks us down, like a hungry wolf,
Eventually catching up, devours us,
Leaving nothing, but itself.

That forgotten, returns,
Haunting us, night and day,
When least suspected, it floods back,
Taking with it, all we seek to protect.

That which we pretend to be,
engraves its name upon us,
for all to see what we have become,
and what we are no longer.

And so turns the karmic wheel,
around and around,
until at last,
its work with us is done.

Why Wait?

Sometimes we get lost, waiting
for things to happen in life.
While waiting,
we miss our joy,
and replace it with worry,
doubt, disappointment, and confusion.

Waiting causes us to wish
for a reality different
than the one showing up.
While waiting for what we want,
we postpone engaging the moment at hand–
the only reality available to us.

Like most bad habits dying hard,
waiting is a vice grip on life,
causing us to miss
what presents itself
and deserves our full attention.
So, why wait?

Friends Who Dare to Love

Walk with me, be my friend,
Continue on, till the end,
And when the road disappears,
Let's sit together, count the years.

Not one forgotten, or let go by,
Each a precious star in the sky,
Then, when each is accounted for,
We open yet one final door.

Through it together, we slowly walk,
Words we hold, do not talk,
Once on the other side of time,
We await the bells, till they chime.

Then through the valley, they echo long,
Fill us deeply with their song,
Throughout the night, our love burns strong,
Our hearts rejoice, forever we belong.

Those Who Watch but Cannot See

They love it—the voyeurs,
those who live by watching.
Vicariously they live, feeding on others,
unable to see themselves,
even when they look in the mirror.

The sun sets suddenly without warning—
A glorious sight, but the voyeurs missed it.
Ever so subtle orange-yellow colors,
like our sweet-smelling first-grade crayons,
that enthusiastically colored outside the lines.

Yes, they missed the sunset,
as their own heartbeat escapes them.
Lurkers, mesmerized by others' stirrings.
Life for them—a spectator sport
to be watched, not played with passion.

Tempted as we are—
we shouldn't watch the watchers,
which would make us just like them—
blind, lifeless, and empty.
To the voyeurs in life—
fill yourself with life.
No need then to simply watch.

Between Worlds

cold dark night
moonlit winter promises
hovering lust, always just beyond
night soon slips away, yet still inside me

morning, a long-distance journey
to awakening
one of remembering
seeing with eyes wide-open

twilight bridges night and day
sunrise comes at last
a journey of color
bright oranges, reds, yellows

a new day begins
yet still I slumber
eyes wide-open
sun shining bright

Winter Meditation

Winter's eve drawing nigh,
Dark clouds hover, January sky,
Fading firelight, flickers gloom,
Dancing barefoot 'cross the room.

Huddled shadows hushing the night,
In your arms, hold me tight,
Sharp-edged snowflakes fall so still,
White frost clings, nearby window sill.

Longing for what's not there,
No comfort found, my rocking chair,
Sitting still, motionless,
Holding on, memories caress.

Brutal cold winter night,
Full moon shining, oh so bright,
Sitting still by the fire,
Surrender there, all desire.

Let Us Pray for Light

While we are created in God's image,
we live as mortal humans,
and therefore we are
vulnerable to our own inner darkness.

Let us pray for Light,
to illuminate our path,
as we walk through
the dark side of our souls.

Whatever This Day Brings, Let Us Be Grateful

We can learn from our pain,
even our fear of lingering uncertainty.
Let's not squander our precious life energy
on creating puzzles, hyperbolic machinations,
and self-destructive nightmares.

Let's seek wisdom from within ourselves,
and use it to live with our own *not knowing*.
Hear the clarion call for self-peace,
putting an end to our self-inflicted suffering.
Whatever the day brings, let us be grateful.

Today is a New Day

Today is a new day—
a chance to heal and start over.
It's a day for removing our cancer,
and our fear, anger, and resentment.

Today is a new day—
an opportunity to see ourselves
and the world
in a fresh healing light.

Today is a new day—
a powerful new starting point
for living fully,
and embracing our wholeness.

Today is a new day—
let's not waste it
on pain and suffering.
Let's live this day with gratitude.

Healing is Everyone's Job

The world is broken,
troubled with deep anger and fear,
causing people and the earth to suffer.

We contribute to the world's suffering
when we act strictly in our own self-interests,
and fail to see how we impact others.

Some people seem to think
it's somebody else's job
to help the world heal.

Why do they think that way?
Maybe suffering is all they know,
and they don't know how to heal themselves.

If we're not healing ourselves
and helping the world to heal,
what are we doing?

Confronting Our Secrets

Everything in life
contains a secret hiding place–
a mysterious storage locker,
where we keep our deepest pain,
darkest fears,
broken promises,
shattered dreams,
false accusations,
shameful thoughts and deeds,
and other desperate acts of survival.

Let's confront our secrets.
Acknowledge their presence,
and remember why we locked them away.
Let's use our secrets
to find our own god of self-understanding,
and help others confront their secrets.
Let's live courageously without secrets.
Let's open the door of our psychic storage lockers,
let the sunlight in,
and chase the mysterious shadows away

Ruminations on Suffering

I keep thinking–
someday we won't suffer so much.
I keep thinking–
someday we'll stop pretending
our suffering can save us.
I keep thinking–
there is life after death,
and life after our suffering.
In each case, we start over,
like the sun rises each morning,
and tears and the rain are reminders
to let go and allow ourselves to flow.

The Power of Change
to Heal

We never know
anything for certain.
But that's not so bad,
because nothing is forever.
And in that light
we see reality,
which escapes us
when we want something different
than what is.
Let's live in the moment,
and never doubt
the power of change to heal us.

Watching a Hummingbird
Snare a Spider

The hummingbird snared and ate the spider–
straight out of the spider's dangling web.
Not something we'd exactly expect
on this pleasant July evening.
But then again,
how much do we really know
about the workings of nature,
let alone the appetite of the hummingbird,
who graces our presence
with his beating wings
and unmistakable humming song?
I hope the spider didn't have plans for the evening.

Returning to Our Virgin State of Wholeness

Sometimes we do things
just to survive–
to avoid our deepest pain,
which may or may not be
of our own making.
And sometimes we do things
just because we don't know
what else to do.

I think back on my life,
and I would encourage you
to think back on yours.
And as we move forward,
let's do things that really matter–
things with the power to transform us,
returning us to
our virgin state of wholeness.

Working Together
for a Cure

Let's close our eyes for just a moment,
and contemplate the miracle of human life.
Nearly forty trillion cells in the body.
Each knows its job,
and each does its job,
in perfect union with all others.
Maybe all of us can work together
to prevent and cure cancer.

Another Way to See
Our Lives

It's easy for all of us
to look at our lives with remorse,
and say I would've, could've, or should've.
We did what we did,
and we didn't do what we didn't do.

Alternatively,
let's gaze upon our lives
with gratitude and forgiveness,
grow our own self-understanding,
and deepen our compassion for others' suffering.

Doing Our Best

Let's do our best
not to be
unwitting hosts
of self-inflicted anger.

Let's do our best
to be
percipient catalysts
of self-directed love.

Cosmic Wisdom
for Cancer

We are not separate
from the whole of life,
despite how we may feel at times.

Like the stars making up the Milky Way,
we give life back to the universe
that gave birth to us.

Because we have life, we have purpose.
We must trust our cosmic instincts
that echo wisdom throughout our beings.

We must trust our Divine purpose.
That is our North Star.
Where there is purpose, there is meaningful life.

When we pray or meditate,
we should allow our North Star
to fill our eyes with stardust

When we speak,
we should allow our hearts to move our lips.
Then our words are real.

When we listen,
we should receive the universe's quantum vibrations.
Then we hear the truth.

And when we lie down to sleep,
let us dream of cosmic wholeness.
For then, we can heal.

Placing Blame Won't Help

We blame our cancer on our family histories,
emotional traumas scarring our bodies and souls,
how we've lived our daily lives,
unwarranted exposure to dangerous chemicals and pollution,
harmful preservatives in the food we love to eat,
all the undue stress and suffering in our lives,
and even a roll of the dice by God.

Like you, I've thought about all these possible causes,
and like you, I'll never know exactly why I have cancer,
and for all of us, placing blame won't make our cancer go away.
And like you, me, and everyone else,
we are impermanent beings that eventually fade away,
so, let's love life, be thankful,
and just do the best we can for as long as we can.

Going Beyond the Limits
of Cancer

Nothing like a clear star-filled night sky
to make you dream,
wander beyond your normal boundaries,
and see previously unnoticed parts of yourself.

Don't let your cancer prevent you
from seeing the magic of a summer night sky,
live your dreams,
or discover new parts of yourself.

Fireworks

Fireworks!
What lights up the sky on the Fourth of July.
What lights up our bodies during radiation therapy.

No matter how sick we are,
we must continue seeing the beauty of life,
and celebrate it with color and music.

Not every day is a picnic,
but each day is precious, because
we know what it is to be alive.

Let's remind ourselves that
we are more–much more–than our cancer.
Each of us is a uniquely beautiful fireworks display!

Reiki on the Cancer Battlefield

Peaceful place on the battlefield,
where cancer cells and chemotherapy go to war.
A restful and rejuvenating oasis,
where a wearied soul refills with life force energy.
A quantum shift in the human biofield,
where waves of possibility bring healing,
and not more cellular destruction.
Comforting a cancer patient with Reiki
in a chemotherapy infusion room.

Breaths at Sunset

Like each breath we take,
no two sunsets are identical.
Like the daily breaths we take,
often we take sunsets for granted.

Like each in-breath we take,
each sunset nourishes our spirits.
Like each out-breath we take,
each sunset helps us to let go.

Tonight's sunset over the lake
reminds me to inhale the beauty of life
with each breath I take,
and never again take a sunset for granted.

Who Am I?

Who am I...
when I stop being afraid,
stop pretending,
give up trying to be somebody, and
finally give in to being me?

I'm not...
the person I thought I was,
wanted to be, or
had to be
to please someone else.

The easiest thing, and
the hardest thing in the world
is being who you are
without trying, and
without being anyone else but me.

All of us stray from ourselves, and
forget who we are.
Next time you lose yourself, just remember
you are the subject, searching
for what you already are.

A Higher Calling

I did better than survive the surgeon's knife,
removing my cancer cells, and
their insatiable appetite for life.
By the grace of God, I was called.
Not home—that unfamiliar place beyond,
but to stay right here, and work with souls
on this side of the mountain.

Journey to the Heart

Wonderful, long-held secrets abound in your heart.
They patiently await you.
Open the door.
Enter with honesty, and
trust whatever that honesty brings.
Discover and unwrap
the many unopened presents,
awaiting you at your heart's door.
Take them inside.
Open each one.
Allow the love they contain to grow.

Rediscover the many gifts of love
that have filled your heart
throughout your lifetime.
Revel in their beauty.
Live in their promise:
that once a gift of love has been given,
it is always with you.

Love is what we all come back to.
For some of us,
it has taken longer
to realize that love is
what we really are.

For some of us,
our entire journey in life
has been about discovering the secrets
that lie buried deep in the cave of our hearts.

It's not a long journey when you're ready.
The heart requires no reservations
to visit what it holds.
Getting there can be as simple as
floating on a lotus blossom
on the still waters of your soul.

A New Path with Heart
Ahead

A new plan ahead for my life–
I feel it brewing in my soul.
Longings first in the mist,
then faint singing voices from afar.
Memories rise, then they fall,
'cross roaming fields of yesterday.

At times, it takes a wake-up call–
Things both strange and familiar–
A sudden brush with death, or even
a child's first sweet whispered words.
Each a sign, a new path ahead–
One filled with heart and soul.

A place I've been before, very long ago.
A partial clearing now in view, and then
a sprawling patch of cheerful wildflowers along the edge
of the narrow winding path, up the hill it goes.
There I stop, in silence listen–
The mournful wail of bagpipes, echoing across the glen.

A new beginning, all this says–
An unknown path with heart calling out to me:

Walk this way in your life,
just beyond what you know.
Fear not, for I will walk with you,
till new feet on this path you grow.

POEM ANALYSIS

"Poetry is the breath of the soul, capturing the whispers of our deepest experiences. By analyzing its verses, we unlock an insight and mindfulness, inviting each word to illuminate the shadowed corners of our consciousness. In this thoughtful examination, our appreciation for poetry deepens, transforming mere lines on a page into mirrors reflecting the intricate tapestry of human emotion and the boundless landscapes of our imagination."
~Don Iannone

In the Poetry Analysis section, we delve into the intricacies of verses found within "Cancer as Spiritual Teacher," exploring the layers of structure, imagery, and meaning that each poem weaves. Poetry, in its essence, is a form of expression that transcends the mere arrangement of words, offering a glimpse into the profound depths of human experience and emotion. Through this analysis, we aim not only to uncover the subtle nuances and thematic threads that bind these poems but also to illuminate how they reflect and articulate the transformative journey of facing cancer. By dissecting the poems' structure, we reveal the scaffolding of thought and feeling upon which they are built. Through imagery, we wander the vivid landscapes of the poet's imagination, landscapes that mirror the tumultuous and enlightening path of illness and recovery. In exploring the meaning, we seek to decode the silent whispers and roaring declarations about life, death, and the spiritual awakening that can emerge from the crucible of suffering.

However, the purpose of this analysis extends beyond mere analysis; it is an invitation. An invitation to you, the reader, to engage with the poetry on a personal level, to find your own reflections within its verses. As we peel back the layers of each poem, consider this a shared journey where your insights and interpretations are as invaluable as those presented on these pages. This collaborative approach does not seek to define the 'correct' understanding of each piece but rather to open a dialogue between the text and the reader. In doing so, we hope to foster a deeper connection not only to the poetry itself but also to the universal experiences of struggle, resilience, and spiritual growth it encapsulates. Through this interactive exploration, may you find not only a deeper meaning in the poems but also a reflection of your own journey and a spark for your own analytical curiosity.

Poem: "On Cancer and Poetry"

Battling cancer, we grasp at every straw,
Poetry, too, becomes a healing salve.
It ushers us gently into life's raw thrall,
Cleansing old beliefs in its restorative bath.

Cancer, those rapids wild, looms in our sight,
But we'll navigate its twists with dignity and might.

Poetry, like life, can dangerously entice,
Revealing depths within us, untouched, unknown.
Yet, in the throes of cancer, it's worth the roll of dice,
For in its verses, a transmuting force is shown.

In the dance with cancer, let poetry play its part,
Transforming our trials into triumph, a healing art.

Analysis of "On Cancer and Poetry"

'On Cancer and Poetry' metaphorically explores the journey of battling cancer and the therapeutic power of poetry. In this poem, cancer is likened to "rapids wild," suggesting a turbulent, chaotic force that the individual must navigate. This comparison evokes the unpredictable and tumultuous nature of dealing with cancer, where one must muster dignity and strength to traverse the difficult path ahead.

Poetry is presented as a healing balm, a soothing and restorative presence in the face of life's "raw thrall," or the intense reality of the cancer experience. It's portrayed as a medium that can cleanse and renew, perhaps by allowing for emotional expression and processing, serving as a form of catharsis.

The poem also touches on the inherent risks of delving into poetry, acknowledging that it can reveal unexplored depths within the self, which can be both dangerous and enlightening. The acknowledgment that poetry can bring to light aspects of ourselves that were previously unknown suggests a transformative potential, aligning with the idea that poetry can lead to personal growth, even when facing something as daunting as cancer.

Finally, the poem suggests that poetry can transform trials into triumph, framing it as a form of "healing art" that assists in the emotional and spiritual journey of the cancer battle. The form of the poem, with its steady rhythm and rhyme scheme, provides a sense of structure and order, offering a counterbalance to the chaos of the subject matter, which reinforces the theme of finding solace and meaning amidst the struggle.

The poem invites readers to consider how engaging with art, in this case, poetry, can be a meaningful and integral part of coping with life's most challenging experiences.

Poem: *"Life Between Our Plans"*

Remember when you were ten,
and thought at twenty-one,
you'd be all grown up and perfectly happy?
Then, when you were thirteen,
your father died of a sudden heart attack,
and your family nearly fell apart.

Remember when you were twenty-one,
and thought at forty,
you'd have life all figured out?
Then, just as you finished college at twenty-two,
you became pregnant with your first daughter Lauren,
and your plans to become a trial lawyer came to an end.

Remember when you were forty-five,
and all three kids were on their own,
and you thought you could launch your writing career?

Then, two days after your first book was accepted,
your mother was diagnosed with Alzheimer's,
and all your life energy shifted to caring for her.

Remember when you were sixty-five,
had published eight books, and you thought
you and your husband Tom could relax and smell the roses?
Then, when you were sixty-seven,
Tom died after a prolonged battle with cancer,
and Lauren entered rehab for drug abuse.

Remember just yesterday, on your eighty-third birthday,
you marveled at how life seems to happen
in between all the plans we make? Nothing could be truer.

Analysis of: "Life Between Our Plans"

The poem 'Life Between Our Plans' reflects on the unpredictability of life and the way it unfolds in contrast to our expectations and plans. It takes the reader through a narrative journey of an individual's pivotal life moments from youth to old age, highlighting the divergence between plans and reality.

At ten, there's a naive anticipation of adulthood at twenty-one, but an unforeseen loss disrupts this view. At twenty-one, there's hope for the future and ambitions of a career, but life takes a turn with the arrival of a child. At forty-five, with newfound freedom and aspirations to write, the protagonist's plans are again upended by a family health crisis. And at sixty-five, when there should be time for leisure and enjoyment, another wave of personal challenges arises.

The poem uses these life milestones to emphasize that while we may have plans, life's true course is often dictated by unexpected events. These interruptions are not merely obstacles; they are integral parts of life that shape our journey.

The structure of the poem, with its repetition of "Remember when," underscores the cyclic nature of anticipation and the ensuing recalibration of life in response to events. This refrain invites the reader to reflect on their own life and the ways in which their plans have been altered by circumstances beyond their control.

The poem suggests a theme of resilience and adaptability, encouraging a philosophical approach to the unpredictability of life. It captures the human experience with poignant clarity, reminding us that life's true substance often lies in the spaces between our plans, in the moments we don't foresee, and in our reactions to the unexpected.

Poem: "Life and Death: Two Sides of the Same Quantum Coin"

Life and death–
Two sides of the same quantum coin.
Heads you win, tails you lose.
Call the flip.
Tails you win, heads you lose.
Call it again.

Life–
What our consciousness manifests
when we flip the coin.
Death–
What our consciousness manifests
when we flip the coin.

Life and death–
Two sides of the same quantum coin.

Analysis of: "Life and Death: Two Sides of the Same Quantum Coin"

The poem 'Two Sides of the Same Quantum Coin' delves into the philosophical and metaphysical exploration of life and death, presenting them as inseparable and interdependent, much like the two sides of a coin in quantum mechanics, where particles can exist in multiple states and possibilities until observed

By invoking the image of a coin flip to represent the randomness and unpredictability of life and death, the poem suggests that these two states are not just opposites but are closely connected, and their outcomes are not as binary as they seem. The repetition of the coin flip and the alternating outcomes challenge the notion of win or lose, suggesting that life and death may be more complex than traditional dichotomies.

The poem also touches on the role of consciousness in the perception of life and death, implying that our understanding or experience of these states may be a manifestation of our conscious minds. This aligns with some interpretations of quantum mechanics, where the observer plays a pivotal role in determining the state of a particle.

Ultimately, the poem encourages readers to think beyond conventional ideas of life and death, considering them not as fixed endpoints but as part of a continuum influenced by our perception and the fundamental uncertainties of the universe. The use of "quantum" emphasizes the modern scientific understanding that reality may not be as clear-cut as it appears, and that there may be more than one way to view the existence and its cessation.

Poem: "Last Time" Awareness

The world looks different to us
with the awareness that
this may be the last time
we will ever see it.

At these times,
goodbyes, no matter how grand,
appreciative, or reverent,
ring with lingering hollowness.

And memories, even the most precious,

become bitter two-edged swords,
reminding us of what we loved,
and what we will never see again.

Even the deepest understanding
of reality's impermanent nature
doesn't prevent us from grasping at
what we love, and what has given us joy.

Analysis of: "Last Time" Awareness

The poem "Last Time" Awareness contemplates the profound shift in perception that occurs when we become aware that we might be experiencing something for the last time. This awareness casts a unique light on the world, infusing ordinary moments with extraordinary significance and a poignant sense of finality.

Goodbyes, regardless of their nature, are depicted as inherently insufficient to encapsulate the depth of emotion felt during these moments. They echo with a sense of incompleteness, suggesting that no farewell can truly encompass the weight of a final parting.

The poem also grapples with the duality of memories. While they serve as cherished reminders of joy and love, they also bring a sharp pang of loss, the "bitter two-edged swords" that remind us of what will be missed. This bittersweet quality of memories highlights the complex emotional landscape of acknowledging a last experience.

Furthermore, the poem reflects on the human tendency to cling to the sources of our joy, despite an intellectual understanding of the transitory nature of life. It speaks to the innate human desire to hold onto the people, places, and experiences that bring us happiness, even in the face of inevitable change or loss.

Overall, the poem is a meditation on the tension between knowing that all things are impermanent and the natural impulse to resist this impermanence when it means letting go of what we hold dear. The theme resonates with a universal human experience—the struggle to accept the transient nature of our existence and the experiences within it.

Poem: "Truth as Your Surgical Knife"

Psychic surgery—
You're the surgeon.
Cut carefully,
removing only the bad,
leaving the good.

Some parts of us look diseased,
needing extrication, but
at a closer inspection, we see
good and bad sewn together.
All parts of the same cloth.

Parts and wholes,
just illusions:
things we hate,
and things we love—
All parts of who we are.

Surgery, on one level,
separating us, parceling out
what's not needed
to be healthy
and grow stronger.

Should you decide
psychic surgery is required
to heal yourself,
choose truth as the knife
to remove what's no longer needed.

Analysis of: "Truth as Your Surgical Knife"

'Truth as Your Surgical Knife' employs the metaphor of psychic surgery to explore the concept of self-reflection and personal growth.

The poem challenges the reader to undertake the difficult task of introspection, using "truth" as a tool to discern and remove negative aspects of the self, much like a surgeon excises unhealthy tissue.

The poem suggests that the process is not straightforward; what may initially appear unhealthy or negative could, upon closer examination, be an integral part of our being. It brings forth the idea that our flaws and virtues are interwoven, making it hard to remove one without affecting the other—indicating the complexity of human nature.

It also touches on the concept that our perception of individual traits is subjective. The "parts and wholes" mentioned in the poem reflect the notion that our qualities cannot be entirely separated from the whole of who we are—they are all connected and contribute to our complete self.

The surgical metaphor extends to the idea of growth, implying that sometimes, parts of ourselves need to be let go for us to evolve and become stronger. The poem concludes with an empowering message, urging the reader to use "truth" as the surgical knife in this delicate operation of self-improvement. Truth becomes the necessary, albeit sharp, tool that helps us cut away the parts of ourselves that no longer serve us well.

Overall, the poem is an insightful reflection on the intricate and often painful process of self-improvement and the pursuit of personal truth.

Poem: "Cancer as Spiritual Teacher"

In every life, lessons are sown,
Truths to unearth, to make our own.
Some are simple, like recipes to taste,
Others, complex, not one bit of waste.

Our souls may shout from depths of pain,
But from such trials, wisdom's what we gain.
With open hearts and minds to blend,

New paths appear, old ways we mend.

To learn from cancer, a task so stark,
Yet within its shadows, a divine spark.
It's a dance of balance, a call to find
Our truest selves, in heart and mind.

The lessons I've learned, humbly so:
To let fear and ego gracefully go.
To tread a path where trust is a must,
And love guides my steps, in the divine I trust.

Cancer is more than its physical trace,
It holds lessons deep, for us to embrace.
With clarity and courage, let's each find,
In spiritual truth, peace of mind."

Analysis of: "Cancer as Spiritual Teacher"

The poem 'Cancer as Spiritual Teacher' delves into the profound and transformative journey of someone experiencing cancer. It suggests that life is filled with lessons, both simple and complex, which shape our existence. The poem's narrative seems to recognize that within the struggle and suffering caused by cancer, there is an opportunity for deep spiritual and personal growth.

The poem is structured to lead the reader through a process of self-discovery and enlightenment, asserting that through suffering ("our souls may shout from depths of pain"), there is potential for gaining wisdom. It emphasizes the idea that embracing these challenges can lead to the healing of the soul and the discovery of one's true self.

The poet speaks of cancer not just as a disease but as an experience that encompasses profound life lessons that are to be embraced and understood. There is a call for courage and clarity to navigate this journey, with the ultimate goal of finding peace of mind in "spiritual truth."

The poem's message is one of hope and resilience, urging readers to trust in a greater power and to approach life with love as their guiding principle. It articulates a perspective that sees cancer not solely as an adversary but as a rigorous teacher with valuable lessons to impart.

This interpretation aligns with the broader themes of finding meaning and growth in the face of adversity, a common thread in many spiritual and philosophical traditions. It resonates with the belief that confronting our deepest fears and challenges can lead to a richer, more enlightened existence.

Poem: "Our Lives as Quantum Questions"

Let's not make unwarranted assumptions in life,
because they block our natural spiritual unfolding.
Far better to allow open questions to linger,
until they are ready to answer themselves.

Each of us is a living question, and
we remain alive as long as our question lingers.
Our questions ride quantum waves of possibility,
until they become answers, then they cease to exist.

Analysis of: "Our Lives as Quantum Questions"

The poem "Our Lives as Quantum Questions" explores the theme of uncertainty and the idea that life is an evolving series of questions rather than fixed states. It advises against hastily forming assumptions, as these can hinder our spiritual growth and the natural progression of our understanding. The poem suggests embracing uncertainty and allowing the space for questions to exist without immediate answers, aligning with the concept that knowledge and wisdom often come in their own time.

By describing each individual as a "living question," the poem implies that the essence of life is to seek, explore, and inquire. This quest for understanding is what keeps life dynamic and evolving. The reference to "quantum waves of possibility" alludes to quantum theory, where particles exist in all possible states until observed. Similarly, the poem conveys that our questions have boundless potential and exist in a state of possibility until they crystallize into answers, at which point they "cease to exist" as questions.

This metaphor may reflect on the human experience, suggesting that answers can sometimes bring closure to the wonder that drives us. In essence, the poem seems to celebrate the state of questioning as a vital and intrinsic part of the human condition, one that should be cherished and maintained for as long as possible.

Poem: "Jigsaw Puzzles in the Cancer Treatment Waiting Room"

Jigsaw puzzles, missing pieces everywhere,
That patients, families, and friends share.
Some they finish, most they don't,
Some too hard, so they won't.

Oddly shaped interlocking and tessellating pieces.
Bit by bit, the perplexing mystery decreases.
Skilled puzzlers work first to build the frame,
While others treat all pieces exactly the same.

Some work the puzzles like their lives,
Trying this, trying that, till an answer arrives.
While befuddled by the jigsaw puzzles,
Cancer causes much bigger struggles.

For some, the puzzles distract them from their pain.
Others wonder about life on the celestial plane.
When finally, the nurse calls their name,
In the waiting room, the jigsaw puzzles remain.

Analysis of: "Jigsaw Puzzles in the Cancer Treatment Waiting Room"

The poem 'Jigsaw Puzzles in the Cancer Treatment Waiting Room' employs the metaphor of a jigsaw puzzle to capture the varied experiences of patients and their loved ones in a cancer treatment waiting room. The incomplete puzzles with missing pieces symbolize the uncertainty and the incomplete picture of life that patients may feel while undergoing treatment.

The act of attempting to finish these puzzles reflects the human need for order and control. Just as skilled puzzlers begin with the frame, some people approach their challenges with strategy and structure, while others may address their problems more randomly or haphazardly, treating "all pieces exactly the same."

The poem also suggests that puzzles provide a form of distraction and a coping mechanism for those waiting, allowing them to focus on something other than their pain or the overarching questions about life and existence ("wonder about life on the celestial plane").

However, the reality of cancer is never far away, as indicated by the interruption of the nurse's call. This represents the ongoing battle with the disease, which overshadows the simple activity of the puzzles. The puzzles, left unfinished in the waiting room, are a poignant image of the transient nature of life and the universal human experience of leaving things undone.

Ultimately, the poem speaks to the shared experience of seeking solace and distraction in small tasks amid larger life struggles and the commonality of this experience among those in the waiting room.

Poem: "Winter Meditation"

Winter's eve drawing nigh,
Dark clouds hover, January sky,
Fading firelight, flickers gloom,
Dancing barefoot 'cross the room.

Huddled shadows hushing the night,
In your arms, hold me tight,
Sharp-edged snowflakes fall so still,
White frost clings, nearby window sill.

Longing for what's not there,
No comfort found, my rocking chair,
Sitting still, motionless,
Holding on, memories caress.

Brutal cold winter night,
Full moon shining, oh so bright,
Sitting still by the fire,
Surrender there, all desire.

Analysis of: "Winter Meditation"

'Winter Meditation' is a contemplative poem that invokes the sensory experiences of winter and a sense of longing or reflection. The poem opens with the onset of a winter's evening, setting a scene that is both calm and somber with its "dark clouds" and "fading firelight." The imagery of "sharp-edged snowflakes" and "white frost" adds to the starkness of the winter landscape, suggesting both the beauty and harshness of the season.

The mention of "dancing barefoot 'cross the room" introduces a sense of vulnerability and perhaps a longing for warmth or comfort, which is echoed in the following lines where the speaker seeks solace in another's embrace, contrasting the cold exterior with a need for human connection.

As the poem progresses, there's a tangible sense of yearning for something absent, with the "rocking chair" serving as a symbol of solace that fails to comfort. The stillness and motionlessness could represent a deep introspection or a paralysis of action in the face of missing what is not present.

The "brutal cold winter night" and the "full moon shining, oh so bright" juxtapose the cold darkness with a glimmer of light, which might reflect on the dual nature of winter as a time of desolation and reflection, but also of clarity and illumination. The closing lines suggest a surrender to the contemplative state, letting go of desires as one sits by the fire, perhaps finding peace in the acceptance of the moment.

Overall, the poem uses the winter setting as a backdrop for exploring themes of introspection, solitude, and the human desire for warmth and connection in the face of life's cold and inevitable absences.

Poem: *"Confronting Our Secrets"*

Everything in life
contains a secret hiding place–
a mysterious storage locker,
where we keep our deepest pain,
darkest fears,
broken promises,
shattered dreams,
false accusations,
shameful thoughts and deeds,
and other desperate acts of survival.

Let's confront our secrets.
Acknowledge their presence,
and remember why we locked them away.
Let's use our secrets
to find our own god of self-understanding,
and help others confront their secrets.
Let's live courageously without secrets.
Let's open the door of our psychic storage lockers,
let the sunlight in,
and chase the mysterious shadows away.

Analysis of: "Confronting Our Secrets"

'Confronting Our Secrets' is a poem that speaks to the universal human experience of harboring hidden aspects of oneself. The "secret hiding place" mentioned in the poem serves as a metaphor for the parts of our psyche where we tuck away our most profound suffering, fears, and regrets. These are likened to a "mysterious storage locker," a vivid image suggesting a contained, dark space where one stores the elements of life that are too painful or uncomfortable to face openly.

The poem suggests a process of healing through the courageous act of confronting these secrets. It posits that by acknowledging these hidden parts, we can better understand ourselves and potentially aid others in their journeys as well. The call to "live courageously without secrets" speaks to the freeing act of opening oneself up to the light of truth, dispelling the "mysterious shadows" that secrets cast over our lives.

The act of letting sunlight into these dark places is symbolic of clarity, exposure, and possibly the warmth of acceptance. It implies a transformative process that can lead to growth and the alleviation of the burdens we carry.

Overall, the poem encourages transparency with oneself and presents this openness as a path to self-discovery and authentic living. It's a call to action to embrace vulnerability and use it as a tool for personal and communal empowerment.

Hanging in Pristine Nakedness

Too often, too much.
At times, not enough.
Then, when we're satisfied,
something new arises,
moving us, to yet another new place,

Usually a place we'd never find, unless
the world slows down enough,

letting us catch up,
letting us surpass ourselves,
and find more truth than lies.

More solid, dependable ground we need
rather than earthquake-shaken soil,
undermining our hope,
dumping us headlong
onto the beach of time.

And then, the beach disappears,
and all her sand is gone,
we're left, hanging
like the new moon,
in pristine nakedness before sunrise.

Analysis of "Hanging in Pristine Nakedness"

The poem "Hanging in Pristine Nakedness" unfolds through a structure that mirrors the ebb and flow of human experience, marked by a rhythm of desire and disillusionment, discovery and loss. Its structure, devoid of a consistent rhyme scheme, instead relies on the natural cadence of contemplation and realization, guiding the reader through the cycles of seeking satisfaction and encountering the inevitable shift towards new desires or truths. This progression from satisfaction to seeking, grounded to unsteady, and presence to absence, underscores the transient nature of life and the constant pursuit of meaning amidst change.

Imagery in this poem serves as a vehicle for conveying the themes of transience, discovery, and vulnerability. The contrasting images of "earthquake-shaken soil" versus "solid, dependable ground" encapsulate the human yearning for stability in a world that is inherently unstable. The "beach of time" and the disappearance of sand invoke the relentless passage of time and the fleeting nature of human achievements and desires. The most striking image, the "new moon, in pristine nakedness before sunrise," evokes a sense of raw vulnerability and new beginnings. This imagery not only paints a vivid picture of the human condition but also invites the reader to reflect on their own experiences of vulnerability and change.

The poem's meaning revolves around the theme of life's impermanence and the human quest for truth and stability amidst this uncertainty. It suggests that true understanding and peace come not from clinging to what we have or what we know but from embracing the continuous cycle of change and self-transcendence. The poem posits that it is only by allowing ourselves to be vulnerable, to "hang" in our "pristine nakedness," that we can truly confront the essence of our being and the reality of our existence. This state of nakedness—of being stripped of pretensions and illusions—facilitates a deeper connection with the fundamental truths of life. Thus, the poem invites readers to accept the inherent instability and uncertainty of life as a pathway to discovering more profound, enduring truths.

CANCER TRENDS AND CARE CARE

> "In the relentless march against cancer, every step forward in treatment and prevention shines as a beacon of hope. With each breakthrough, we not only push the boundaries of science but also kindle the flames of possibility for countless lives touched by this formidable adversary."
> ~Don Iannone

Cancer in the United States: A Persistent Health Challenge

Cancer continues to pose a significant health challenge in the United States, representing a major cause of morbidity and mortality among the population. Despite considerable advances in medical science and treatment strategies, cancer remains the second leading cause of death in the U.S., following heart disease. The American Cancer Society's estimates for 2023 highlight the ongoing impact of this disease, projecting over 1.9 million new cancer cases and more than 600,000 cancer deaths within the year. These figures underscore the persistent burden cancer places on individuals, families, and the healthcare system at large.

Breast, lung, prostate, and colorectal cancers are among the most diagnosed cancer types in the U.S., contributing significantly to the overall cancer incidence. Lung cancer, in particular, accounts for the highest number of cancer-related deaths, a statistic that reflects the aggressive nature of the disease and the challenges associated with its late detection and treatment. The prevalence of these cancers and their impact on mortality rates highlight critical areas for continued research, prevention efforts, and early detection initiatives.

The burden of cancer is not shouldered equally across the U.S. population, with disparities in cancer incidence and outcomes evident among different demographic groups. Factors such as socioeconomic status, race, and access to healthcare services play a crucial role in these disparities, affecting cancer risk, the stage at diagnosis, treatment received, and overall patient outcomes. For example, African American men have higher rates of prostate cancer incidence and mortality compared to men of other racial and ethnic groups, underscoring the need for targeted prevention and treatment strategies.

In response to the ongoing challenge of cancer, significant resources are being invested in research aimed at understanding the disease's mechanisms, developing new treatments, and improving cancer prevention and early detection methods. Public health initiatives focusing on reducing risk factors such as smoking, obesity, and sedentary lifestyles are also central to the effort to lower cancer incidence and mortality rates. Furthermore, advancements in personalized medicine and immunotherapy are opening new frontiers in cancer treatment, offering hope for more effective therapies with fewer side effects.

Despite these efforts, cancer remains a formidable adversary in the realm of U.S. public health, demanding continued vigilance, research, and investment to reduce its impact and improve outcomes for those affected.

Advances in Cancer Care

The journey of cancer treatment has evolved dramatically from its rudimentary beginnings to today's era of sophisticated, targeted approaches. Historically, the primary modalities for cancer treatment were surgery, chemotherapy, and radiation therapy. While effective for many patients, these methods often came with significant side effects and a one-size-fits-all approach that did not account for the unique nature of each patient's cancer. In recent decades, however, we've witnessed a paradigm shift towards more personalized and less invasive cancer care methodologies, fundamentally changing the landscape of cancer treatment and patient outcomes.

One of the most significant advancements in the field of oncology is the development of targeted therapy. This treatment modality focuses on specific molecules and cell mechanisms crucial for cancer cell growth and survival, offering a more precise approach compared to traditional chemotherapy. Targeted therapies can block the growth and spread of cancer by interfering with specific molecules involved in tumor growth and progression. As a result, they often have fewer side effects, significantly improving the quality of life for patients undergoing treatment.

Immunotherapy represents another breakthrough in cancer care, harnessing the power of the body's immune system to fight cancer. By stimulating or restoring the immune system's ability to detect and destroy cancer cells, immunotherapies have shown remarkable success in treating a variety of cancer types. These treatments, including checkpoint inhibitors and CAR-T cell therapy, have revolutionized the prognosis for many cancers that were previously considered untreatable, offering hope to patients with advanced and hard-to-treat cancers.

The advent of precision medicine has further personalized cancer treatment, tailoring therapies based on the genetic makeup of an individual's cancer. This approach has enabled oncologists to select treatments that are most likely to be effective and minimize side effects, based on a detailed understanding of the cancer's biology. Precision medicine's ability to identify genetic mutations and alterations in cancer cells has led to the development of therapies that target those specific changes, significantly enhancing treatment efficacy and patient survival rates.

The Role of Artificial Intelligence (AI) in Cancer Diagnosis and Treatment

Artificial Intelligence (AI) has emerged as a transformative force in healthcare, with its integration into cancer care marking a significant leap forward in diagnosis and treatment. AI algorithms can analyze vast amounts of data quickly and with high precision, aiding in the early detection of cancer and the identification of novel treatment pathways.

In the realm of diagnosis, AI applications such as imaging analysis, pathology, and genetic testing are revolutionizing how cancers are detected and classified. AI-driven imaging analysis can identify subtle patterns in medical images that may be indicative of early-stage cancer, often before it's visible to the human eye. Similarly, in pathology, AI algorithms can analyze tissue samples for cancerous changes with a level of detail and accuracy surpassing traditional methods. Genetic testing, powered by AI, allows for the rapid sequencing and analysis of genetic material, identifying mutations that may increase the risk of certain cancers or influence treatment choices.

AI's capability to process and interpret complex data is also enhancing treatment planning and the personalization of cancer care. By integrating patient data, including genetic information, AI can help predict how individual patients will respond to various treatments, guiding oncologists in creating personalized treatment plans that are optimized for each patient's unique cancer profile.

Looking forward, the potential future developments of AI in oncology are vast. AI is expected to further refine the accuracy of cancer diagnoses, identify new targets for treatment, and enhance the precision of personalized medicine. It could also play a crucial role in monitoring treatment response and predicting cancer recurrence, making it an indispensable tool in the continuous effort to improve cancer care and patient outcomes.

These advancements in targeted therapy, immunotherapy, precision medicine, and the role of AI in oncology represent just the tip of the iceberg in the evolving field of cancer treatment. As research continues and these technologies advance, the future of cancer care looks increasingly promising, with the potential to save more lives and offer a better quality of life to those affected by cancer.

The Integration of Complementary Medicine with Conventional Cancer Treatment

As the landscape of cancer care evolves, a notable shift towards a more holistic approach to cancer care has emerged, blending conventional treatments with complementary therapies to address not just the physical but also the psychological and emotional needs of patients. Leading cancer centers like the Cleveland Clinic Cancer Center, MD Anderson, Mayo Clinic, Johns Hopkins, Memorial Sloan Kettering, and Dana-Farber are at the forefront of this transformative movement, advancing research and care practices daily to incorporate a broader spectrum of patient care methodologies.

Institutions like the Cleveland Clinic Cancer Center offer programs in Reiki, massage, reflexology, art and music therapy, yoga, esthetician services, mindfulness, peer mentoring, patient education, and nutrition, recognizing the significant impact these practices can have on a patient's overall well-being. MD Anderson has a dedicated Integrative Medicine Center where patients can access acupuncture, physical therapy, and nutritional counseling alongside their medical treatments. These leading centers understand that treating cancer is not just about targeting the disease itself but also about nurturing the patient's mental and emotional health, aiding in their recovery and improving their quality of life.

Research initiatives conducted by these prestigious institutions have shown promising results in the efficacy of complementary therapies. For instance, studies at Mayo Clinic have found that mindfulness and meditation can significantly reduce symptoms of anxiety and depression in cancer patients, while art and music therapy sessions at Memorial Sloan Kettering have been credited with lowering levels of pain and stress. Dana-Farber has published findings on the benefits of nutrition and physical activity in not only aiding recovery but also in reducing the recurrence of certain types of cancer.

These centers are also leading the way in educating healthcare professionals and the public about the benefits of an integrated approach to cancer care. Through workshops, seminars, and published research, they advocate for a care model that includes Reiki, massage, reflexology, and other wellness services as standard adjuncts to conventional cancer treatments. This approach helps patients cope with symptoms more effectively and experience greater peace, calm, and comfort during their treatment journey.

The commitment of these institutions to advancing integrated cancer care practices underscores a fundamental shift in how cancer is treated. It recognizes the patient as a whole being, addressing the complex interplay between body and mind in the healing process. As research continues to unfold, the hope is that more cancer centers worldwide will adopt this holistic approach, making complementary medicine an integral part of cancer care and patient recovery.

POETRY THERAPY

Poetry is finding its place in cancer care and medicine more broadly. This section discusses how poetry therapy is playing a more active role in patient care in all realms of medicine.

Poetry therapy is a form of expressive arts therapy that employs the reading, writing, and sharing of poetry as a means to promote emotional healing and growth. It operates under the premise that poetry can help individuals express feelings and experiences that might be difficult to articulate through conventional conversation. The therapeutic process of engaging with poetry allows individuals to explore their inner thoughts, feelings, and experiences in a structured yet creative manner, facilitating insight, personal growth, and healing.

The practice of poetry therapy can involve several activities, including:

- **Reading poetry**: This can help individuals find words and images that resonate with their experiences, providing comfort, validation, and insight..
- **Writing poetry**: The act of writing allows indi-

viduals to articulate their own thoughts and feelings, which can be cathartic and enlightening.

- **Sharing poetry**: Whether sharing their own work or poems by others that they find meaningful, individuals can feel less isolated in their experiences and more connected to a community.

Poetry therapy is utilized in a variety of settings, including hospitals, hospice facilities, mental health clinics, schools, and community centers, and can be beneficial for people of all ages dealing with a wide range of issues, from mental health challenges like anxiety and depression to life transitions, grief, and coping with illnesses like cancer.

Professionals trained in poetry therapy may include psychotherapists, counselors, social workers, and educators, who integrate this approach into their practice to support their clients' or students' emotional and psychological well-being. The National Association for Poetry Therapy (NAPT) provides guidelines and training for those interested in becoming registered poetry therapists or poetry therapy facilitators.

The Value of Poetry Therapy in Cancer Care

In the realm of cancer care, where patients and their families navigate the complexities of diagnosis, treatment, and the emotional upheaval that accompanies this journey, poetry therapy emerges as a source of solace and catalyst for expression. This therapeutic approach, which involves the reading, writing, and sharing of poetry, offers a unique pathway to coping with the myriad of feelings and experiences triggered by cancer. It serves not just as a form of escapism but as a practical tool for healing, understanding, and connection.

Poetry therapy provides a voice to the often inexpressible emotions that both patients and their family members face. The metaphoric and symbolic language of poetry allows individuals to articulate their fears, hopes, and grief in ways that conventional language might not permit. This form of expression can lead to significant emotional releases, offering relief from the bottled-up emotions that can exacerbate stress and pain. For cancer patients, writing or identifying with poetry can be particularly empowering, enabling them to reclaim their narrative from the clutches of their disease.

Moreover, poetry therapy facilitates a deepened self-awareness and introspection, guiding patients and families through the process of self-discovery and reflection. It encourages the exploration of one's inner world, leading to insights that can enhance coping strategies, resilience, and emotional well-being. For many, poetry becomes a mirror reflecting their innermost selves, helping them to confront and understand their feelings and fears about illness, mortality, and loss.

The shared experience of poetry also fosters a sense of community and connectedness among cancer patients and their families. Poetry therapy sessions, whether conducted in support groups, workshops, or one-on-one settings, create a safe and inclusive space for expressing vulnerabilities and shared experiences. This communal aspect of poetry therapy can break down feelings of isolation and alienation, offering comfort in the knowledge that others share similar struggles and emotions. Through the shared language of poetry, patients and families can find mutual support, understanding, and a sense of belonging.

Beyond emotional support, poetry therapy also contributes to cognitive stimulation and mental agility. Engaging with poetry can enhance cognitive function, improve memory, and provide a mental diversion from the rigors of cancer treatment. For family members, poetry offers a constructive outlet for coping with caregiving stresses and the emotional toll of watching a loved one battle cancer.

In essence, poetry therapy is a holistic tool in cancer care, addressing the psychological, emotional, and social dimensions of coping with the disease. It validates and gives voice to the silent fears and hopes of those affected, while also building a supportive community rooted in shared experiences and expressions. As research and practice in this area continue to grow, the incorporation of poetry therapy into comprehensive cancer care programs underscores the recognition of healing beyond the physical, embracing the profound interconnectedness of body, mind, and spirit.

The Integration of Poetry Therapy in Leading Cancer Care Centers

Poetry therapy has found its place among innovative therapeutic approaches within several prestigious medical centers across the United States, highlighting its growing recognition as a valuable component of cancer care. Institutions such as the University of Southern California (USC), Harvard Medical School, Massachusetts General Hospital, and the UCSF Medical Center are pioneering the integration of this expressive therapy into their oncology departments and supportive care programs. These centers acknowledge the impact that poetry therapy can have on enhancing the quality of life for patients undergoing cancer treatment and their families.

At the University of Southern California, poetry therapy is part of a broader initiative to incorporate the arts into healing, recognizing that creative expression can significantly benefit emotional and mental health. USC's innovative approach to patient care emphasizes the importance of addressing the psychological and emotional aspects of cancer treatment, alongside the physical.

Harvard Medical School and its affiliated hospitals, including Massachusetts General Hospital, have also embraced poetry therapy, incorporating it into their psycho-oncology and palliative care services. These sessions offer patients and their families a unique outlet for expressing their feelings, facilitating a deeper understanding of their emotional responses to cancer and fostering a sense of community among participants.

The UCSF Medical Center, known for its comprehensive cancer care and research, offers poetry therapy workshops as part of its integrative medicine program. These workshops are designed to support patients and family members in exploring their experiences through poetry, providing a therapeutic space for reflection, expression, and connection.

The adoption of poetry therapy by these and other leading medical institutions signifies a shift towards more holistic cancer care models that value the therapeutic potential of the arts. By integrating poetry therapy into their programs, these centers are offering patients and their families innovative ways to navigate the emotional landscape of cancer, promoting healing, resilience, and a sense of empowerment.

As poetry therapy continues to gain momentum in the field of oncology, it stands as a testament to the evolving understanding of what constitutes effective, compassionate care. Through the power of words and the shared human experience they convey, poetry therapy is helping to transform the journey of those affected by cancer, offering solace and strength in the face of adversity.

Broader Perspective of Poetry Therapy

In the exploration of poetry's role within the nexus of medical humanities and clinical care, its application as a healing modality, particularly in palliative and hospice medicine, is garnering increased attention. Poetry therapy, as delineated by the National Association for Poetry Therapy and further supported by the Institute for Poetic Medicine, emerges as a significant approach for addressing grief, loss, and enhancing resilience among patients and clinicians alike. This modality leverages the unique capacity of poetry to access and articulate the complex tapestry of human emotions, facilitating a profound connection to one's inner experiences and fostering a sense of community and understanding among those navigating the challenges of serious illness.

The implementation of poetry therapy within healthcare settings, including palliative care environments, serves not only as a conduit for emotional expression and processing but also as a means for clinicians to engage with their own experiences and reflections. The act of poem-making and sharing within a supportive community enables both caregivers and patients to explore meanings, relationships, and the often-unacknowledged aspects of clinical practice. Amidst the heightened emotional landscapes prompted by the COVID-19 pandemic, the value of such creative and reflective practices has become increasingly evident, underscoring the necessity for supportive spaces that facilitate emotional processing and resilience through artistic expression.

Despite the apparent benefits and growing implementation of Poetic Medicine programs across various healthcare settings, the field faces challenges related to isolation, lack of consensus on program definitions, and the need for more rigorous evaluation methodologies. The development of a proposed framework aims to standardize the role and impact of poetry in healthcare, outlining three primary approaches: poetry reading as community ritual, facilitated poetry writing workshops, and poetry's integration into healthcare education. Notable programs, such as those conducted by the UCSF/MERI Center and the Jesse Brown VA Medical Center, exemplify the diverse applications and profound impact of Poetic Medicine, offering insights into its potential to enhance well-being, foster empathy and resilience, and address the multifaceted needs of patients and healthcare providers alike.

In summary, the integration of poetry therapy within the healthcare continuum represents a promising avenue for enhancing holistic care, offering a unique lens through which patients and clinicians can explore and express the intricacies of the human condition. As the field continues to evolve, further research and collaborative efforts will be essential in solidifying Poetic Medicine's role as a vital component of compassionate, patient-centered care.

Don Iannone's poetry has inspired, comforted, and entertained readers and listeners since the early 1990s. "Cancer as Spiritual Teacher" is his most popular poetry collection, which was first published in 2018. Because of its popularity, Don committed himself to a rewrite of the book, adding new poems, rewriting many existing poems, and including analyses of ten poems in the book. Don serves as a faculty member at Transcontinental University. He and his wife, Mary, provide complementary medicine services to patients at the Cleveland Clinic Cancer Center. Don is the author of twenty-four books that cover non-fiction, poetry, and photography. Born in the steel and coal regions of Eastern Ohio, Don's early life in Martins Ferry and St. Clairsville lends a genuine depth to his life story. He and his wife live in Chagrin Falls, Ohio. Don holds doctorates in Divinity and Philosophy. Learn more about Don at: https://www.donaldiannone.com/

Analogy in poetry: A comparison between two different things, suggesting they are alike in some way.

Art therapy: A therapeutic technique that uses the creative process of making art to improve a person's mental health and well-being.

Artificial intelligence (AI): The simulation of human intelligence in machines that are programmed to think like humans and mimic their actions.

Camino de Santiago: A network of pilgrimages leading to the shrine of the apostle Saint James the Great in the cathedral of Santiago de Compostela in Galicia in northwestern Spain.

Cancer stages: A way to describe the size of a cancerous tumor and how far it has spread from where it originated.

Cleveland Clinic Taussig Cancer Institute: A part of the Cleveland Clinic in Ohio, known for cancer care and research.

Clinical caregiver: A healthcare professional who provides direct care and support to patients, especially in clinical settings.

Complementary medicine: A range of medical therapies that fall beyond the scope of scientific medicine but may be used alongside it in the treatment of disease and ill health.

Dana-Farber: The Dana-Farber Cancer Institute, a leading cancer treatment and research center in Boston, Massachusetts.

Dr. Eric Klein, MD: Former urologic surgeon at Cleveland Clinic.

Dr. Harry Isaacson, MD: Internist and Executive Dean of Cleveland Clinic Lerner Medical School.

Eckhart Tolle: A spiritual teacher and author known for his works on personal growth and spirituality.

Expressive arts therapy: A multimodal therapeutic approach that may include music, dance, drama, and visual arts to promote emotional growth and healing.

Form in poetry: The structure of a poem, including its rhyme scheme, meter, stanza structure, and line lengths.

Free verse poetry: Poetry that does not rhyme or have a regular meter.

Haiku: A traditional form of Japanese poetry consisting of three lines with a syllable pattern of 5-7-5.

Harvard Medical School: One of the world's leading medical schools, part of Harvard University in Boston, Massachusetts.

Hospice: Care that focuses on the palliation of a terminally ill or seriously ill patient's pain and symptoms.

Iannone, Donald, T., Ph.D., D.Div., An American author of poetry, nonfiction, and photography books. He serves on the faculty of Transcontinental University, and he is a complementary medicine consultant to Cleveland Clinic's Taussig Cancer Center in Cleveland, Ohio.

Imagery in poetry: Descriptive language in a poem that engages the senses and paints a picture in the reader's mind.

Immunotherapy: A type of cancer treatment that helps your immune system fight cancer.

Institute for Poetic Medicine: An organization that promotes healing through poetry.

Integrative medicine: Combines traditional Western medicine with alternative or complementary treatments, such as acupuncture or massage, for holistic care.

Johns Hopkins: Johns Hopkins University is renowned for its medical school, hospital, and public health programs, located in Baltimore, Maryland.

Kim Bell, RN, MBA: Chief Administrative Officer of Taussig Cancer Institute at Cleveland Clinic.

Lyric poetry: A short form of poetry expressing personal feelings or emotions, traditionally sung.

Massachusetts General Hospital: A top-ranked hospital providing comprehensive healthcare, and a teaching hospital of Harvard Medical School.

Mayo Clinic: An American nonprofit academic medical center focused on integrated clinical practice, education, and research.

MD Anderson: The University of Texas MD Anderson Cancer Center, a comprehensive cancer treatment and research center in Houston, Texas.

Medical humanities: An interdisciplinary field that applies humanities disciplines (like literature, philosophy, ethics, history, and religion) to medical education and practice.

Memorial Sloan Kettering: A world-renowned cancer treatment and research institution in New York City.

Metaphor in poetry: A figure of speech that describes an object or action in a way that isn't literally true but helps explain an idea or make a comparison.

Meter in poetry: The rhythmic structure of a verse or lines in verse, typically defined by the pattern of stressed and unstressed syllables.

Mindfulness: The psychological process of bringing one's attention to experiences occurring in the present moment.

Music therapy: A therapeutic approach that uses music to address physical, emotional, cognitive, and social needs of individuals.

Narrative poetry: Poetry that tells a story and has a full storyline with characters, a setting, and a plot.

National Association for Poetry Therapy: An organization that promotes growth and healing through poetry and related expressive arts.

Palliative care: Specialized medical care for people living with a serious illness, focused on providing relief from symptoms and stress.

Patient education: The process by which health professionals inform and educate patients about their health conditions and treatment options.

Peer mentoring: Support given by one person to another who has similar characteristics or circumstances.

Poetry: A form of literature that uses aesthetic and rhythmic qualities of language to evoke meanings in addition to, or in place of, the prosaic ostensible meaning.

Poetry analysis: The examination of the elements and structure of poetry to understand its meaning and themes.

Poetry therapy: The use of poems to promote healing and growth.

Poetry types: Various genres and forms of poetry, each with specific features, such as sonnets, haikus, and free verse.

Precision medicine: An approach to patient care that allows doctors to select treatments that are most likely to help patients based on a genetic understanding of their disease.

Primary site cancer: The original location where a cancer tumor first developed before possibly spreading.

Psych-oncology: A field of interdisciplinary study and practice at the intersection of psychology and oncology, focusing on the psychological aspects of cancer.

Reflexology: A therapy that involves applying pressure to specific points on the feet, hands, or ears, with the aim of benefiting other parts of the body.

Remission: A period during which symptoms of disease are reduced (partial remission) or disappear (complete remission).

Rhyme poetry: Poetry that uses rhyme, a repetition of similar sounds in two or more words, often at the end of lines.

Spiritual psychology: The study and practice of the human experience in relation to a higher power, spiritual beliefs, and practices.

Structure in poetry: The organized pattern or sequence of lines or stanzas in a poem.

Tanka: A genre of classical Japanese poetry and one of the major genres of Japanese literature.

Targeted therapy: Drugs or other substances that block the growth and spread of cancer by interfering with specific molecules involved in tumor growth and progression.

Therapeutic massage: A type of therapy that involves the manipulation of soft tissues in the body to relieve pain, help heal injuries, improve circulation, relieve stress, increase relaxation, and aid in the general wellness of clients.

Thomas Merton: An American Trappist monk, writer, theologian, mystic, poet, social activist, and scholar of comparative religion.

Thomas Moore: A psychotherapist and writer who integrates spirituality and psychology, known for his bestselling book "Care of the Soul."

UCSF Medical Center: The University of California, San Francisco Medical Center, a highly-ranked hospital system known for its research and treatment.

University of Southern California (USC): A private research university in Los Angeles, California with strong programs in many fields including medicine and the arts.

Yoga: A group of physical, mental, and spiritual practices or disciplines that originated in ancient India.